SAGITTARIUS

November 22–December 21

T0066045

Image by Andrea Lauren © Simon & Schuster, Inc.

✧ Mark Twain ✧

Image by Andrea Lauren © Simon & Schuster, Inc.

Images by Andrea Lauren © Simon & Schuster, Inc., and 123RF/Volodymyr Horbovyy

CARNATION

Image by Andrea Lauren © Simon & Schuster, Inc.

Image by Andrea Lauren © Simon & Schuster, Inc.

Sagittarius
I am
READY
FOR
ADVENTURE

Images by Andrea Lauren © Simon & Schuster, Inc., and 123RF/Volodymyr Horbovyy

Images by Andrea Lauren © Simon & Schuster, Inc., and 123RF/Volodymyr Horbovyy

Image by Andrea Lauren © Simon & Schuster, Inc.

autumn

Image by Andrea Lauren © Simon & Schuster, Inc.

Sagittarius

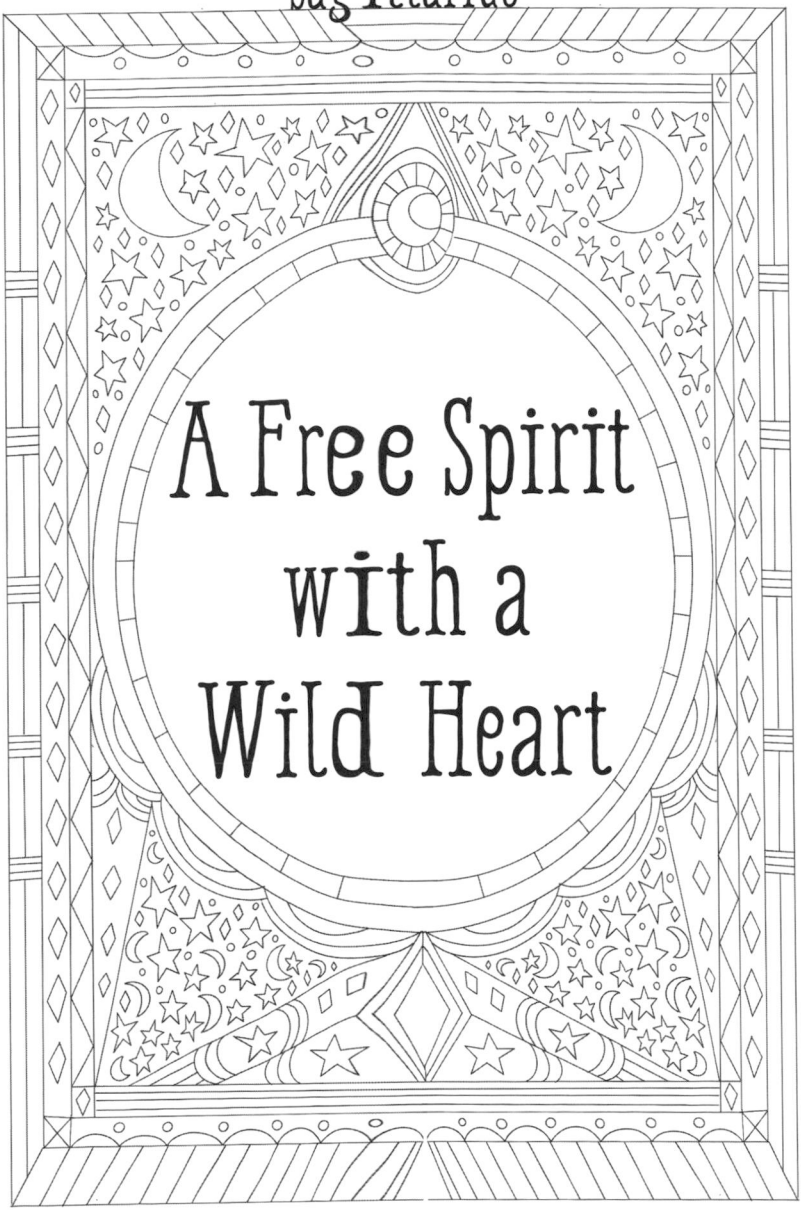

Image by Andrea Lauren © Simon & Schuster, Inc.

Sagittarius
4
Ruled by Jupiter

Image by Andrea Lauren © Simon & Schuster, Inc.

Sagittarius

Image by Andrea Lauren © Simon & Schuster, Inc.

ADVENTUROUS
ORIGINAL
Charismatic
INDEPENDENT
Philosophical

Image by Andrea Lauren © Simon & Schuster, Inc.

Images by Andrea Lauren © Simon & Schuster, Inc., and 123RF/Volodymyr Horbovyy

Image by Andrea Lauren © Simon & Schuster, Inc.

RULING
HOUSE
9
The House of
Philosophy

Image by Andrea Lauren © Simon & Schuster, Inc.

SAGITTARIUS
Whatever I set my sights on I go after

Image by Andrea Lauren © Simon & Schuster, Inc.

Images © 123RF/Volodymyr Horbovyy and Getty Images/KavalenkavaVolha

Images by Andrea Lauren © Simon & Schuster, Inc., and 123RF/Volodymyr Horbovyy

Image by Andrea Lauren © Simon & Schuster, Inc.

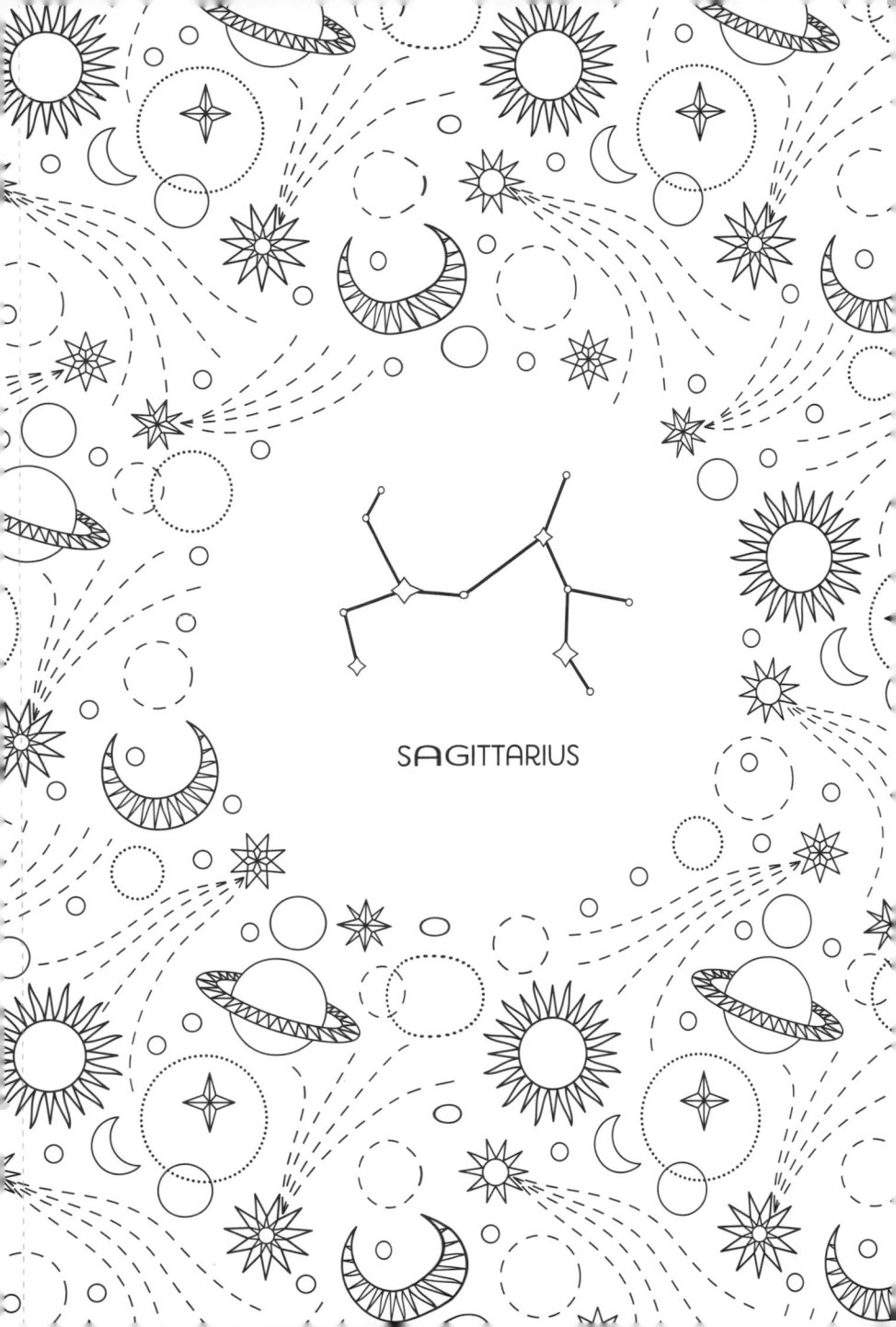
SAGITTARIUS

Images © Getty Images/ElenaLux and 123RF/kotoffei

Aries
Taurus
Gemini
Cancer
Leo
Virgo
Libra
Scorpio
Sagittarius
Capricorn
Aquarius
Pisces

Images by Andrea Lauren © Simon & Schuster, Inc., and 123RF/Volodymyr Horbovyy

Fire Signs

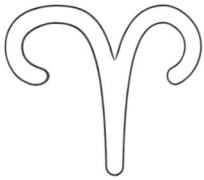

Aries

Leo

Sagittarius

Images by Andrea Lauren © Simon & Schuster, Inc., and 123RF/Volodymyr Horbovyy